74b

L B̄RP.

Georgina von Etzdorf

Georgina

NILGIN YUSUF

Georgina von Etzdorf

Sensuality, Art, and Fabric

WATSON
GUPTILL

First published in 1998 in the United States of
America by Watson-Guptill Publications, a division of
Billboard Publications, Inc.,
1515 Broadway, New York, NY 10036

Library of Congress CIP data applied for.

ISBN 0-8230-1147-X

This book was conceived,
designed, and produced by
THE IVY PRESS LTD
2/3 St Andrew's Place
Lewes
East Sussex BN7 1UP

Art Director: Terry Jeavons
Design and page layout: Alan Osbahr
Photography: Guy Ryecart
Commissioning Editor: Christine Davis
Managing Editor: Anne Townley

Printed and bound in Hong Kong

Contents

Georgina

Jonathan

Martin

"Life should hold purpose and delight for everyone. Art and Design have the capacity to deliver both, providing we understand how we are touched by each. In all of us there is a rhythm to which we have the freedom to respond. Its energy, source, beauty, and complexity is a mystery. But its spirit can communicate that the industry of one's life should match the rhythm of it. Then we are enriched by the depth and delight that we discover. Our purpose becomes illuminated, lighting up our dreams and illustrating the road ahead. Art, design, print, fabric, color, texture, movement, light, beauty, quality, vitality, freedom; this is not work, it is the way of life we choose to live. Enrichment through artistry. Inspired by living."

Georgina von Etzdorf, Jonathan Docherty, Martin Simcock

Introduction

SOMEWHERE AMONG the smart shoppers of Sloane Street, London, wedged between the elegant designer stores, is a nondescript doorway and set of buzzers. If you press one of them and walk upstairs, you find yourself drawn out of the monochrome bustle into a place of brilliant color and sumptuous sensuality. It could be an art gallery or bohemian salon; paintings are hung on the wall and a chaise longue is scattered with velvet slippers and cushions. But this is a showroom, where buyers come to place orders with Georgina von Etzdorf—a label that for 17 years has produced some of the finest and most inventive hand-printed textiles in fashion.

Internationally respected, Georgina von Etzdorf has built an empire largely on one item: the scarf. Transformed from mere finishing touches that enhance an outfit into wondrous statements in their own right, Georgina von Etzdorf scarves radiate, resonate, reverberate. Brilliantly colored and patterned, and fashioned in a wealth of fabrics from lustrous velvets and metallic silks to the finest cashmeres and chiffons, these are canvases for the neck, music made cloth.

Unlike designer scarves that promote wealth or status, a Georgina von Etzdorf creation expresses sensuality and individuality. It delights the eye, feeds the senses, and fires the imagination. Although these individual accessories remain the company's proud symbol, seen glistening around the necks of Hollywood and royalty, at the Oscars or fashion awards, the label has diversified greatly since its beginnings in 1981. A full range of clothing and accessories has been added to the lyrical repertoire: delicious opera coats and robes, fluid and fluttering bias-cut dresses, footwear, millinery, and an interiors range of pillows and kilims. Georgina von Etzdorf is now exploring new forms of design and decoration including embroidery, beading, and constructed multi-media textiles. But whether the final product is a printed silk-satin striped robe, a hand-beaded organza stole, or a rich velvet devoré bolster, a distinctive handwriting marks out Georgina von Etzdorf's work from that of many other fashion and textile companies. On the surface is richness, vitality, depth, and subtlety. Beyond this is intelligence, integrity, purpose, and vision.

Three-way partnership

Although the company bears one name, it is the result of a three-way dynamic. Georgina von Etzdorf, Martin Simcock, and Jonathan Docherty are the textile triumvirate who, since the beginning, have steered the organization creatively, practically, and commercially. As the company has grown, the partners' roles have at different times merged, separated, polarized, and evolved. Georgina von Etzdorf, whose signature has become the house

"Ten years ago, people would come in and ask for a scarf. Now, it has to be a Georgina von Etzdorf scarf."

Printed silk chiffon scarf, 1994.

Velvet bouclé scarf, 1997.

8

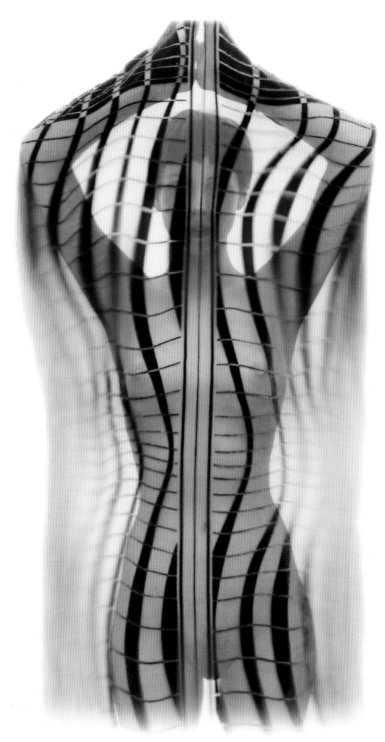

logo, has nevertheless always been the artistic eye. As artistic director, Etzdorf heads the design team and oversees the distinctive look of the collections. Etzdorf studied textile design in the 1970s alongside Martin Simcock at Camberwell School of Art in London. Simcock in the past has directed Sales and Merchandising and is currently head of the Research and Development department, which explores new materials and processes, seeking out innovative routes to take the company forward.

Jonathan Docherty, who studied industrial design at Central School of Art, had been a friend of Simcock since teenage years. After a two-and-a-half year period of post-graduation traveling together, Simcock and Docherty made contact with Georgina, who had been developing her own designs in between unsuccessful freelancing. The three started producing print designs together and became increasingly absorbed by their work. With his industrial design background Docherty went on to play a key role in design development and business coordination. Since 1990, his official role has been that of managing director, guiding the business side of the company.

Humble beginnings

Georgina von Etzdorf products are available in 21 countries and 400 outlets worldwide, including a shop in London's Burlington

Left: Velvet devoré scarf, 1997.
Below: Cotton velvet robe, 1990.

Printed rayon velvet slippers, 1997.

9

Arcade and an outlet in New York's ultimate department store, Barney's. Sixty-five percent of the company's output is exported and there are agents in London, Paris, New York, Milan, Munich, and Tokyo. Sales flourish in stores such as Liberty of London, where Georgina von Etzdorf has increasingly come to dominate the accessories department and has visibly inspired a whole new generation of textile-turned-fashion designers to create accessory collections. "Ten years ago, people would come in and ask for a scarf. Now, it has to be a Georgina von Etzdorf scarf," observes Sue Holmes, head accessories buyer at Liberty. Inspiring fierce devotion in fans across the globe, these sophisticated collections have surprisingly humble roots, which only adds to their charm and authenticity.

It all started in 1978, when Etzdorf's parents donated the use of a garage and stable block at their home in Great Cheverell, Wiltshire, as a temporary printing area. With only their ideas, the most rudimentary printing equipment, and a $800 donation from the Crafts Council, Etzdorf, Simcock, and Docherty began to experiment. Wooden screens were handmade, dye was blended in a Kenwood kitchen mixer, and fabric dried off with a hair dryer.

As orders gradually emerged—from Yuki, J.&M. Pallant and Caroline Charles—the company slowly spluttered into gear.

In 1983, with the help of a $48,000 government loan, the partners rented a nineteenth-century flint-coursed barn and later a stable block in the grounds of a Queen Anne manor house in a village outside Salisbury, Wiltshire. This remains the location for all of the company's screen printing, color dyeing and sampling. Set apart from city life, this rural milieu is the spiritual and cultural heart of Georgina von Etzdorf. A glass-fronted building overlooking the serene Chalke Valley is the base for quality control, distribution, warehousing, administration, and accounts. The rustic setting is in direct contrast to the sales showroom, design studio, and press office situated in the heart of London. In addition to these are the commission contractors who hand-dye and "devoré" the Georgina von Etzdorf collections, and the hundreds of outworkers who machine, hand-stitch, hand-roll, hand-knot, tassel, fringe, and label all the scarves.

The emphasis on hand-printing and production, which some would criticize as an anachronism, has had a stabilizing effect on Georgina von Etzdorf's gradual but assured ascension. This is a

View of the Chalke Valley, Wiltshire; inset: the Georgina von Etzdorf headquarters.

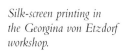

Silk-screen printing in the Georgina von Etzdorf workshop.

"You have to nurture ideas. Everything we do has a reason, purpose, and spirit."

company that has grown not in proportion to demand, but directly in relation to output capacity. The limitations were clear, and from the start orders were only taken for what it was possible to produce and deliver. "In the beginning we had planned to be a design house, creating prints for designers," recalls Simcock. This was never to be. At that time, commission printers could not —or would not—produce their work, and the company was effectively forced into becoming a design and production house.

Influencing directions

The Georgina von Etzdorf design philosophy is one that has elevated craft, made art accessible, and changed our perceptions of what print and pattern can be. Relentlessly experimental, Georgina von Etzdorf relishes the challenge of tackling unexplored fabrics and textures, pushing materials and techniques to their limits, and printing on the supposedly unprintable. As original thinkers and textile pioneers, the trio's influence on modern fabrics has been immense.

The most obvious example of Georgina von Etzdorf's influence in the fashion world today is the widespread use of velvet. First used by Georgina von Etzdorf in 1985, with the designs Fritillary and Large Dragons, the fabric was treated like a canvas with rayon, cotton, and silk velvets hand-dyed and printed in an audacious combination of shades. This uninhibited use of color and print, which flickered and danced on the surface, redefined the nature of velvet.

With a sophisticated eye and painterly hand, this fabric was transformed from a precious evening fabric into luxurious daywear, its success epitomized by the winter 1990 "Stormy Weather" collection. The oncoming decade would see velvet emerge as a fabric staple of designer collections, in due course interpreted with enormous commercial success by the high street stores, where it continues to dominate across all sectors. Indeed, so huge has been the demand for velvet, that there is currently a worldwide shortage.

Velvet was closely followed by, and often combined with, devoré, first used by Georgina von Etzdorf in 1993. A decorative printing process with historical roots, devoré involves the pile of a fabric being burned out—literally devoured—using a chemical substance. Traditionally employed in moderation on velvet, devoré was adopted and advanced by Georgina von Etzdorf, making it something new and exciting. Extremely intricate, with most of the pile eliminated and the pattern separated by fragile veins of fabric, the principles of color, movement, and depth were translated into this rediscovered technique, transforming each piece into something mercurial and mysterious.

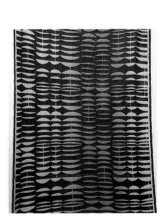

Metallic devoré scarf, 1997.

Degradé print chiffon, 1997.

Viscose satin devoré scarf, 1996.

Rayon velvet shawl, 1993.

Georgina von Etzdorf has tirelessly explored devoré's possibilities, applying it to unexpected fabrics with unpredictable and usually influential results. Exquisitely worked on silk, satin and metallic viscose, rayon fur, chenille, and wool bouclé, its surprise popularity has spurred mass-manufacturers into finding cheaper ways to produce the distinctive semiopaque/semitransparent technique. Devoré scarves and shirts have now become a decorative classic of modern eveningwear.

As well as elevating the humble scarf, Georgina von Etzdorf has also made a major contribution to the revival of men's accessories. As strutting front-runners of the peacock revolution in the early 1980s, alongside designers such as Scott Crolla and Georgina Godley, the company applied its vibrant hallmark to traditional male clothing. Men may have long been regarded as the more subdued sex, but Georgina von Etzdorf chose to ignore the demarcation lines to offer a range of unrestrained velvet waistcoats, crêpe de Chine cravats, silk jersey evening scarves, and jacquard ties.

Perhaps Georgina von Etzdorf's main contribution, however, has been to change people's perceptions, rather than their wardrobes or homes. Through an uncompromising use of color, texture, and pattern, the collections have introduced to the traditionally sober British palette the delights of rhythm and richness, sensuality and sophistication—qualities probably once regarded as too flamboyant for the average Anglo-Saxon. The common sense of commercial taste was questioned, and the reply has been resounding.

Art, industry, and design

The fashion business, with its relentless system demanding fresh ideas every six months, can wear out even its most energetic innovators. But since the early 1980s Georgina von Etzdorf has managed to maintain a vivid identity and self-contained dignity. This design company reflects its own values, beliefs and passions, with collections which evolve organically. Unlike many other prints, which instantly reveal their fashion "moment," Georgina von Etzdorf's creations resist easy cataloguing. They are never out of fashion, because they were never strictly "in" fashion. They are beyond fashion.

Georgina von Etzdorf steers clear of the fashion industry's built-in obsolescence, founded on instant gratification and rapid boredom. Instead, designs are valued for their own sake

Assorted printed silk ties, early 1980s.

"I am vehement about the quality of something created by hand. That is what gives the work its vitality and movement."

Velvet smoking jacket with printed silk lining, 1989.

Reverse silk jacquard waistcoat, 1987.

Degradé print spun silk shirt, 1993.

and expected to endure a lifetime, not six months. This philosophy is best illustrated by the fact that archive designs are often reworked over years and through different collections. Using alternative colorways, proportions, repeats, layers, or processes, each interpretation gives the original print a fresh lease of life. This "aesthetic recycling" complements the constant stream of new ideas, giving both depth and integrity to the collection as a whole. "You have to nurture ideas. It's about a natural evolution. Everything we do has a purpose and spirit," believes Simcock.

Blurring the distinction between art and design, the free-form, open-minded approach has more in common with past fine artists who have worked on fabric—such as Sonia Delaunay or Raoul Dufy—than with other fashion textile houses who design according to market needs or current trends. The designs for Georgina von Etzdorf's fluid prints start life as paintings, executed in watercolors, gouache, or chalk. The hand-drawn line and the loose, considered brushstroke have always been favored over the slick imagery of conventional print design. Etzdorf herself is first and foremost an artist. The desire, evident in every collection, to "liberate" cloth—via color, pattern, and texture— is the result of an irrepressible and highly original talent, one that

could have chosen canvas but, fortunately for the fashion world, opted for fabric. The partners are well aware of what makes their work so distinctive. Docherty has an apposite definition: "If you can take it apart brick by brick, it's design; if you can't, it's art." Etzdorf is firmly placed in the latter category.

At Georgina von Etzdorf, art is intrinsically linked with craft —a movement that has gained increased kudos in the 1990s. An arts and crafts revival, evident across all disciplines from furniture to fashion, has elevated and ennobled hand processes. As machines and computers become increasingly proficient, it is left to artists and craftspeople to show the depth and originality of the human spirit, the skill and individuality of the human hand. "I am vehement about the quality of something created by hand," declares Etzdorf. "That is what gives the work its vitality and movement."

As both a laboratory for ideas and a sympathetic environment allowing creativity and cross-fertilization, the Georgina von Etzdorf design studio and workshop represent a strand of British artistic culture that can be traced back to the Omega Workshops earlier this century, and to William Morris. From small creative communities, great things grow. Every scarf, every pillow and robe is essentially a hand, reaching to a hand.

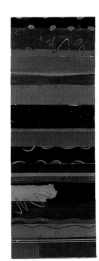

The original sketch for Ridgeway design, left, emerges as the Parallel design, right, from 1977.

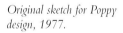

Poppy design in repeat, 1978.

Original sketch for Poppy design, 1977.

Breaking the borders

LOOK CLOSELY at any Georgina von Etzdorf product and you will experience the inanimate come alive, the silent become almost audible. Often in unexpected color combinations and with several contrasting visual elements, Georgina von Etzdorf's creations have their own energy and life-force: you can almost see them pulse, hear them hum. The more you look, the more you see, and all the while the piece draws you in, asking to be touched.

Before Georgina von Etzdorf, fashion's printed textiles had traditionally meant the floral or the figurative. While there had been many brilliant designers, colorists, and masters of fabrication, most prints were ultimately governed by an unyielding production system that spawned endless motifs and static, undemanding designs. Whether the source of inspiration was neoclassical or medieval; whether the pattern was derived from flowers, butterflies, suns, or doves, the motifs and images were tirelessly borrowed and reproduced, their references obvious. Designs might be arranged wittily or impressionistically, generously or sparingly, expanded or reduced, juxtaposed or repeated. But ultimately most would end up flat and two-dimensional, firmly contained in the spaces defined by body shape and production methods, with little or no relationship to the fabric. "When we started, the feel of fabrics was terribly static, with no flow or rhythm," recalls Etzdorf. "We tried to combat the idea of two-dimensional surfaces and develop something new and different. We wanted to create a seamlessness and fluidity which, rather than act as an interesting distraction, would take the eye on a journey."

When the company was first established, the partners attempted to work with commission printers. These large firms, mainly based in the north of England, were paid by designers and textile companies to translate their designs into cloth. It was here that Etzdorf, Simcock, and

PRISM
Design for a border,
fall/winter 1992

The Georgina von Etzdorf "croissant" symbol emerges from within this geometric design. The symbol came about accidentally when Etzdorf was trying to write her signature with a dip pen. To encourage the ink flow she scratched out a shape—and a most unusual logo was born, one that breaks all the rules of company branding. *Left*: the "croissant" cast in bronze, by Margaret Turner.

DRAGONS
Silk crepe-back satin square, spring/summer 1984

Full of movement and energy, the design appears to flow beyond the borders, encroaching upon the edges and breaking out of the top left-hand corner. This refusal to be intimidated by the borders of fabric is one of the elements that make Georgina von Etzdorf's designs so distinctive.

SMALL DRAGONS
Silk twill tie, spring/summer 1984

Although Dragons was reduced in scale for use on men's ties and scarves, it still retains its swirling fluidity.

STAR WARS
Original sketch and printed chiffon square, 1981

Star Wars was the first Georgina von Etzdorf design to be featured on the cover of *Vogue*. *Above*: one of the original sketches from which the design emerged.

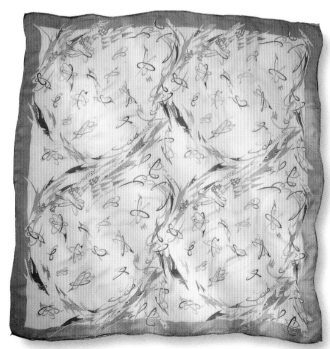

Docherty came up against the many, varied, and restrictive rules of the print establishment, primarily devised to prevent fabric wastage. They were told that diagonals and horizontals added cost to production, that flat images and multi-directional prints were easier and cheaper to re-create than textural, one-directional ones. The establishment dictated that a print should not have too many colors, or use shapes that were too detailed or difficult. "We wanted to explore beyond these limits but were turned away by the commercial printers," recalls Docherty.

It was the inflexibility of commercial print-ers that effectively forced Etzdorf, Simcock, and Docherty to set up their own print facilities, which in time would prove to be an invaluable creative and practical advantage. The poor quality of color matching was another reason to go it alone. "Color is fundamental to our work and we were always particular," says Etzdorf. "Printers would often offer a 'commercial match'—which meant that we submitted an emerald green colorway and were sent a forest green one back." At Georgina von Etzdorf—where the design process is explored at every level from fabric choice to making the screen, applying the dye, and plotting repeats—print contractors could not offer the necessary time or freedom to develop the creative possibilities.

Away from the constrictions of contract printers, Etzdorf, Simcock, and Docherty were afforded the time to play, invent, and question. Although the company's early years were marked by austerity, they were matched equally

QUILLS
Original designs and silk square

The original watercolor sketch for Quills, *below left*, is translated into a complete art work in repeat, *below*. A deceptively simple screen design, it was devised to work effectively on squares and lengths of fabric. In order to print lengths, the borders were masked out; to print squares, they were left in. *Opposite*: Quills on a silk crêpe de Chine square.

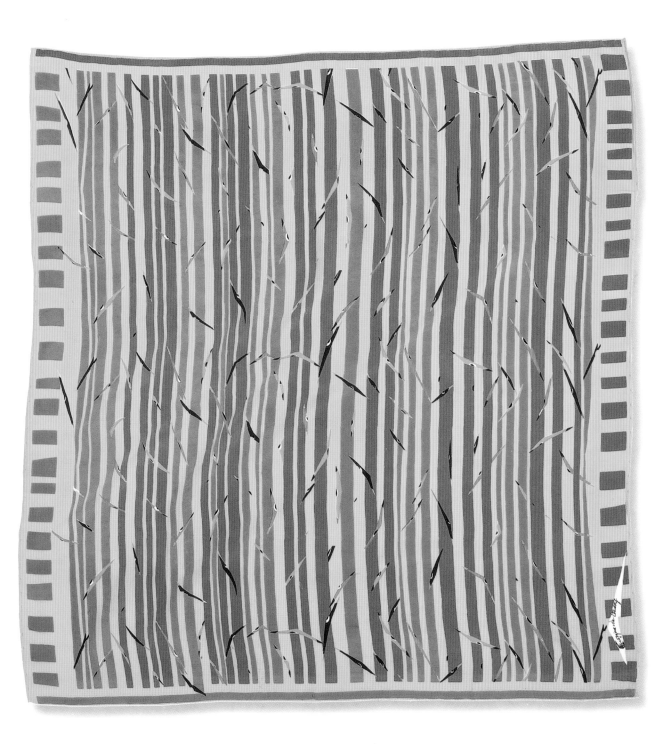

17

by fresh thinking, flexible ways of working, and original solutions. Freed from creating designs to suit machinery specifications, they could produce short, exclusive runs and devise manufacturing techniques to enhance, rather than obscure, the design process. "Manufacturing is an integral part of the design process, supporting and stimulating it," insists Simcock.

The basic rules of repeat design were among the first to be questioned. How might a repeat print not look like a repeat print? How could one create a flow that would take the eye through the cloth on a never-ending path? Docherty, with his industrial design background and technical expertise, played a key role in finding ways to make these goals a reality. "We spent a lot of time developing the use and size of repeat printing and breaking out of the normal repeat method, trying to move beyond the edges of the design," he recalls. "If a repeat threw up a diagonal, we would try to use that as an advantage. One, composed of an inverted mirror image, took three weeks to crack—which we finally did at 3 o'clock on a Sunday morning in an empty, leaking Macclesfield mill. We called that design 'Purgatory.'"

Subtle differences, unexpected additions, and uneven sections were mischievously tossed into repeat prints, giving energy and life. Many

METROPOLIS
Men's wool scarf, 1981

One design can go a long way at Georgina von Etzdorf. The original repeat design for Metropolis, *right*, was first created as a five-screen print, seen here on one of the first men's scarves.

METROPOLIS
Spun silk cravats, 1981

The design shown opposite is transformed by using only three of the screens *(far left)* and one screen *(left)*. The Metropolis three-screen design was renamed Zig-Zag.

PURGATORY
Detail from crêpe de Chine square, 1984

The aim of this notoriously complicated design was to disguise the repeat—an apparently straightforward exercise but one which required ingenuity and creativity. The final effect, resembling shards of fragmented glass, is intriguing and perplexing.

DRAGONFLY
Long chiffon scarf, spring/summer 1993

The Zig-Zag design, which emerged from Metropolis, is enlarged to become Dragonfly, part of the "Dragonflies Draw Flame" collection.

designs involved the dye being applied directly to the screen with a brush, rather than a conventional squeegee, giving a sense of depth and spontaneity. A whole range of colors was used at once and because the hand played such a key role, no two prints were ever the same.

Indeed, the partners' refusal to be intimidated by the conventions of print design is also reflected in the company's attitude to color. The fearless forays into the spectrum, for which Georgina von Etzdorf is internationally recognized, reveal an artist's eye for subtlety and inventiveness. The economic restraints of the early years gave an unexpected opportunity to exploit a unique color palette. Due to the high

JUPITER
Original drawing and
silk crêpe de Chine fabric
detail, fall/winter 1997

This ethereal, three-dimensional design was created with a mixture of dye and clear gum, which was applied by hand directly to the screen.

NEPTUNE
Printed silk habotai,
fall/winter 1985

Using a combination of hand-drawn fine lines, swirling movement and inverted or mirrored elements, this technically challenging print effectively disguised its repeat device. The air-blown simplicity of the image belies its complex conception, an approach that combined the organic and the mathematical.

Gloves are an unexpected choice for print designers, primarily because of their fiddly shape and complex form. But Georgina von Etzdorf's painterly designs are here shown to work on small areas as well as large expanses of cloth.

cost of screen development, numbers were limited. This resulted in fewer designs but a wealth of possibilities for colorways, with daring combinations that paid no heed to commercial tastes or fashion trends.

Before setting up with Simcock and Docherty, Etzdorf's print career had not been smooth—she was even fired by one print studio for being uncommercial. "Designers were employed by print studios to churn out five designs a day. George would take up to two weeks to get one out and then they were described as too strong," recalls Simcock. There was no established aesthetic framework or obvious market for these abstract, geometric, and painterly designs inspired by Klee, Hiroshige,

23

Georgina von Etzdorf have experimented with printing on a variety of surfaces including leather, suede, and even wood, seen here on this mahogany-veneered MDF screen.

and Calder. Most clients found it difficult to envisage how they could possibly work in the context of fashion. But what failed to spark the imagination on paper was transformed once it found its way onto cloth, and enhanced still further when converted into clothing.

Whether rewriting the rules of print production or design, a pioneering spirit has always prevailed at Georgina von Etzdorf. Resisting conventions, challenging expected design solutions, and finding alternatives have been fundamental to the company's growth. "You can print on anything so long as it's flat enough," believes Simcock, which is what Georgina von Etzdorf has done with energy, creativity, and skill: on wood, suede, mohair, fur, bouclé, tweed, metallic silk, and bi-elastic velvet which distorts the pattern. When the company started printing on silk chiffon, it was considered a risky venture. If it had been left to the preconceptions of the industry, Georgina von Etzdorf would not have emerged as today's unique voice. "If we had gone down the conventional path, we wouldn't have got very far. You have to be prepared to risk failure rather than not try."

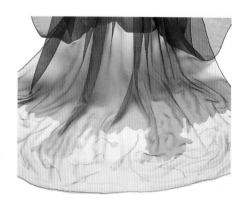

VOLARE
BORDER
Degradé-printed
border on shot
chiffon, spring/
summer 1995

Individual elements of earlier designs will often be drawn out and reinterpreted. This scarf used the border screen from the original Volare design, conceived a year earlier.

COMETS
Printed silk net scarf,
spring/summer 1986

The confidence with which
Georgina von Etzdorf approach
fabrics is illustrated in this early
design which boldly tackles the
finest silk net. Not only is this a
luxury fabric, prohibitively priced,
but it is also difficult to work with
because of its extreme delicacy.

ROSAMUNDI
Discharge printed bi-elastic
velvet scarf, fall/winter 1993

The rich, sumptuous texture of
bi-elastic velvet creates particular
problems. The material tends
to shrink during steaming and
washing, and has to be stretched
when printing and retracted
when dry. Each velvet scarf
demands 50 percent more
work than flat fabric.

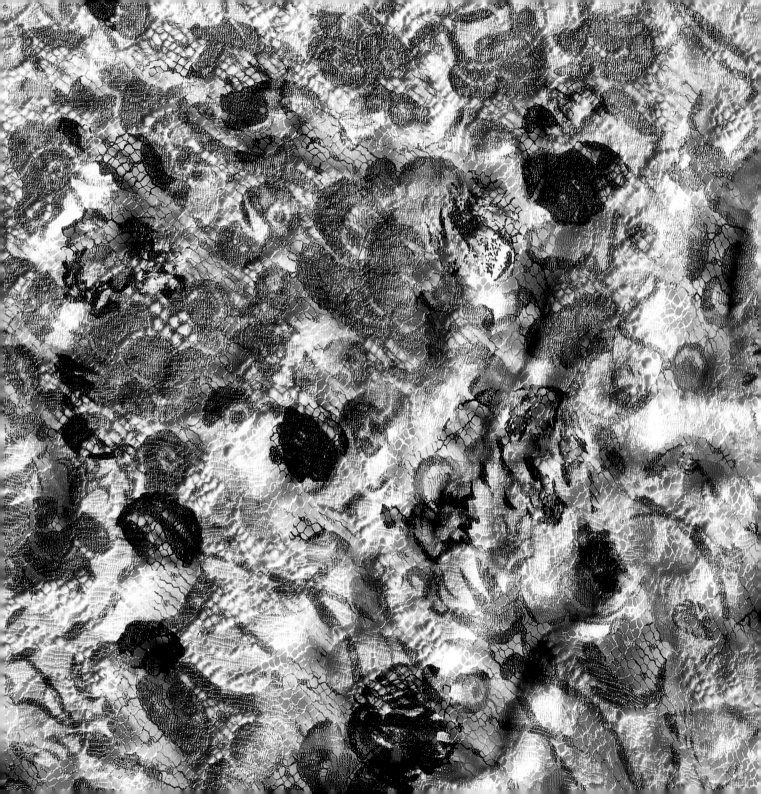

RANUNCULUS
Printed pure silk lace,
spring/summer 1995

The finest lace does not
intimidate the designers at
Georgina von Etzdorf, who
use intricate textures as a
foundation for modern
heirloom pieces.

JETTY
Printed satin-stripe chiffon,
spring/summer 1993

By hand-blending dyes
directly on the screen, a whole
range of subtle gradations
and three-dimensional effects
is achieved—qualities further
enhanced by the seemingly
rippling striped fabric.

SPELLBOUND
Printed silk chiffon,
fall/winter 1994

A swirl of entangled color
is achieved with discharge
printing. This floating,
fluttering design is shown in
three different colorways.

OYSTER
Silk-stripe lace scarf,
spring/summer 1992

A complex and delicate
silk-stripe lace was used
as a basis to explore the
forms of fossils and shells
in this scarf, created for the
"Dancing Ledge" collection.
The vertical lines of the
fabric add a dimension of
movement, while hand-
knotted tassels add weight
to the flyaway fabric.

FROM THE THREE contrasting characters at the helm of the company to its schizoid geographical locations straddling both rural countryside and swish metropolis, contrast and diversity are two elements that underlie many aspects of Georgina von Etzdorf. A company with roots in the Arts and Crafts movement finds itself at the cutting edge of fashion and at the heart of industry; a design label that comes up with fresh collections every six months also produces classics of enduring beauty; while the collections themselves satisfy the intellectual and the sensualist, the bohemian and the modernist alike.

The ordered and exclusive air of Georgina von Etzdorf's retail environments belies the character of the company's key individuals, who are both energetic and wholesomely unpretentious. This is a company that works hard and plays hard. Numerous imaginative and wild themed parties have gone down in the company's history. One was based on the "January Uprising of the Tidpit Cossacks," another was 1940s-inspired and featured a surprise air raid with fake mortar bombs. "One year," recalls Docherty, "we organized a vampire Christmas party. The bus 'mysteriously' broke down on the way to a secret venue, and the terrified passengers were led to a solitary church which was suddenly full of smoke and deafening organ music."

Although the trio have shared interests, including a love of travel and literature, the fact that each personality is very different must contribute to the company's inherent contrasts and contradictions. Etzdorf is the artist among them. Sparkling, expressive, humorous, and articulate, she sings, enjoys South American music, and plays the ukelele ("it can be lively and fun or full of pathos," she maintains). To recharge her creative batteries she will disappear to India for several weeks at a time. She is also

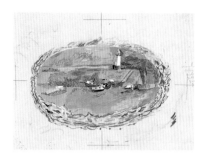

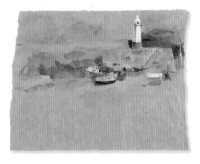

NEWLYN HARBOR
Original artwork and sketches, 1983

One design may be the complex combination of a whole variety of memories and references. The watercolors and sketches above are of Newlyn Harbor in Cornwall, England, where Etzdorf and Simcock both spent vacations. Although painted purely for pleasure, years later they would emerge as part of the "Wish You Were Here" collection of spring/summer 1990.

NEWLYN HARBOR
Original watercolor painting

Another affectionately observed study by Georgina von Etzdorf. The series of paintings illustrates how art can eventually transmogrify into design.

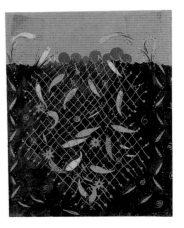

FISHES
Design on paper, 1980

An abstract interpretation of fish caught in a net, this design was never produced in its entire form but inspired the border of the Newlyn Harbor design, *left*.

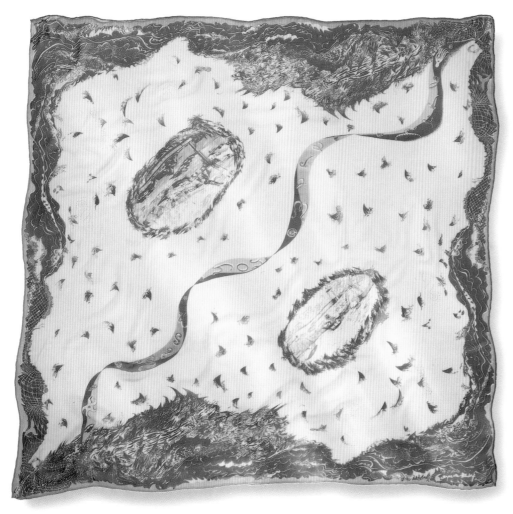

NEWLYN HARBOR
Printed chiffon square, spring/summer 1990

One scarf contains the five separate elements seen on this page and opposite. A witty take on the vacation souvenir scarf, the finished design features the Newlyn Harbor sketches floating on either side of a diagonal ribbon, with other details embedded all around. In contrast to more abstract collections, "Wish You Were Here" promoted a narrative, figurative theme which conveyed the joy and freedom of faraway places.

passionate about Indian miniatures: "I love the way they are made and composed, so rich, image within image, border within border. The colors are sumptuous and the quality of painting remarkable." Jock Gallagher, the non-executive chairman of Georgina von Etzdorf, sees her as "intense as only the highly creative are. She is enormously gregarious and outgoing, which is reflected in her work."

Simcock, who comes originally from Ince, an eleventh-century village in the shadow of Stanlow oil refinery, describes himself as "a mixture of anarchist and conservative." This is reflected in his range of interests which span a passion for rave and dance music, horse-riding, hunting, and going on walking vacations in Patagonia. His love of music started in the days of Wigan Casino and the northern soul underground and continues to this day—he still occasionally DJs in clubs and bars. His role as head of Research and Development straddles two disciplines. "While he is an innate designer, he

The energy and exuberance of Georgina von Etzdorf's designs can be traced right back to their earliest sources. Her sketchbooks are constantly being filled with artistic doodles: colorful characters, costume ideas, places, patterns, and intriguing marks. They reveal the raw elements of an aesthetic, the inner rhythms and patterns inside the designer's mind.

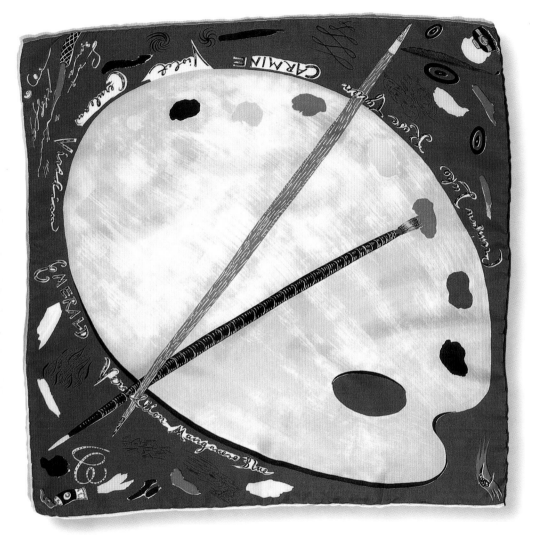

VERMILION
Silk twill bandanna,
spring/summer 1997

**Evocative pigment names
and the painterly image of
an artist's palette combine
to create this signature scarf
in the "Vermilion" collection,
subtitled "A Tribute to
Colour through Cloth."**

EXPLODING WAVE
Discharge print on shot silk organza
shawl, spring/summer 1996

**A degradé print design is used to
highlight the borders of this shawl.
The delicate wispy patterns contrast
with the bold use of shocking pink.**

31

recognizes the need to be ahead of the rest,' notes Gallagher. "He is energetic, restless, inquisitive, and never satisfied."

Docherty, who originally trained as an industrial designer, has quietly turned himself into a businessman. As managing director he is self-contained, organized, and, believes Gallagher, "suited to the discipline of the bottom line." In his spare time Docherty is a keen sailor, hill climber, and cross-country bike rider who owns three motor bikes including a Sunbeam and a Husqvarna. A fan of opera and jazz, he listens to Bellini and Roy Ayers and will routinely escape from spreadsheets and figures to northern Catalonia, the Pyrenees, or Barcelona. Although Docherty presents an exterior of self-effacing charm, Simcock—who has been friends with him since they were teenagers—perceives him to be the most ambitious of the three.

This unlikely trio, who have a tendency to tug in different directions, produce what they like to call "creative conflict." When tensions build, it is usually Gallagher who keeps them apart. "They have a close-knit, terrifically powerful relationship which means they can have spectacular rows, almost like a marital thing. But they are fiercely loyal to each other, dramatically sparking off each other's creativity." The regular tussles and moments of friction that have peppered the company's development bring a vitality to the work that is ultimately a constructive and positive force. "There will be sudden flare-ups over small details. It's a creative tension," believes Gallagher.

COMPASS
Fine linen scrim shawl,
spring/summer 1995

One of a number of purely abstract designs. Making full use of the degradé effect, color and form are employed to create a flow of movement.

ILLUSION
Cashmere silk shawl,
fall/winter 1994

A study in the perception of color: graduated planes against solid blocks give depth and tone, and reduce the solidity of the shapes.

COMPASS
Original paper design,
spring/summer 1994

Contrasts play a central role in many Georgina von Etzdorf prints. Here, light plays against dark, straight against curved.

SPIRE
Shot silk chiffon scarf,
fall/winter 1997

Abstract compositions add an unexpected dimension to the Georgina von Etzdorf stable.

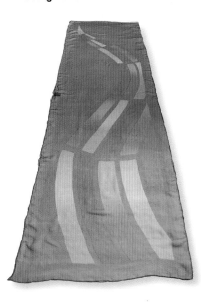

32

NIRVANA
Silk chiffon satin-stripe shawl,
spring/summer 1997

**These geometric studies use a
combination of color, print, and fabric
to create vibrant optical effects.**

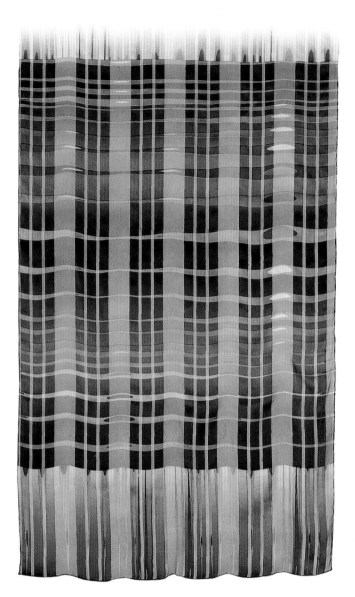

HORIZON
Silk chiffon satin-stripe shawl,
fall/winter 1997

**The wavy horizontal lines of the print
are enhanced by the chiffon's satin
stripes. The overall illusion is one of
restless, humming movement.**

Hand-painted silk shawl,
spring/summer 1995

**Delicate, transparent silk
is hand-painted with the
finest feather brush strokes.**

TRIPLE
METALLIC SILK
Stole, fall/winter 1985

**Three layers of glistening,
highly lustrous metallic
silk form the basis for this
most opulent of stoles.**

FRITILLARY
Reverse-print jacquard
silk pyjamas,
fall/winter 1985

**A wide range of textures
and fabrics is employed at
Georgina von Etzdorf, each
giving a different character
to the finished print.**

SILK METALLIC
POLYAMIDE
Fortuny pleated shawl,
spring/summer 1995

**Gleaming silk metallic
polyamide lends itself
to pleating, which takes
on a sculptural quality
when worn.**

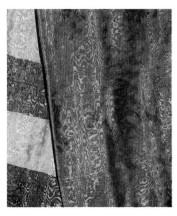

As can be expected from an international company that has sprung from a tiny cottage industry, there have certainly been growing pains. A professional management drive, which aimed to turn the company's creators into managers, is now regarded as a mistake. A disillusioned Simcock disappeared to Chile for three months to recover from a deluge of paperwork, administration, and formal reporting. Etzdorf found she was channeling less energy into the collections; "I could feel the split in my brain," she recalls. Eventually it was concluded that each had their own special role and that these contrasts should be defined and capitalized upon, rather than blurred and integrated. "The industry of one's life should match the rhythm of it," concludes Simcock.

Contrasts are a recurring theme throughout the Georgina von Etzdorf collections. These have swung from the abstract ("Dancing Ledge," "Rhythm & Blues") to the figurative ("Wish You Were Here," "Hide & Seek"), and have often combined elements of both. While the luxury of opulent fabrics such as sheer silk organza, silk jersey, crêpe de Chine, georgette, and fine hand-painted velvet has become the hallmark of Georgina von Etzdorf, "poor" fabrics such as rougher wools and soft linen scrims also play an important role. These have been around since the spring 1994 "Volare" collection, when Simcock introduced the humble linen-and-cotton coarse open-weave scarf. "I wanted something less reverential and precious; something that I could wear myself," he recalls. More recently, mohair, bouclé, chenille, alpaca, and lace have been incorporated into the collections. Whereas other companies are known for a particular house style, Georgina von Etzdorf, with its love of innovation, has experimented with numerous print processes and decorative techniques—including print devoré, discharge, bonding, degradé, flocking, beading, and embroidery.

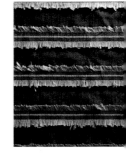

SILK RAFFIA
Detail from scarf,
spring/summer 1995

Apparently disparate fabrics—here, silk and raffia—are often combined to create striking effects.

TASSELLED
LINEN SILK
Detail from scarf,
spring/summer 1996

Tiny rows of tassels stitched onto lustrous linen silk give an extra layer of textural interest and movement.

PRINTED
MOHAIR
Detail from scarf,
fall/winter 1985

Printing on dense, fluffy mohair gives an impressionistic and dream-like effect.

SILK AND
METAL
Detail from stole,
spring/summer 1996

Silk and metal are blended to create a modern, luxurious fabric, also used as a gleaming base for some of the first beaded designs.

35

The winter 1998 collection, "The Prince and the Pauper," characteristically pulls together two opposing themes. One half of the collection is rich, embellished and ornamented in metallic silks and lush brocades; the other is more rustic and hand-worked, using fabrics that are slubbed and nubbly with crochet and handmade effects. "We're trying to create layered levels of texture and taste," says Etzdorf. Indeed for her, designing is no different from cooking. "When you cook a meal, it's not just a visual recipe but a textural and sensual one," she maintains. "Contrasts bring out the richness of what you can offer; variety makes you appreciate the different aspects inherent in each product."

Invitation from the fall/winter 1993 collection

The winter 1993 collection, entitled "The Fire and the Rose are One"—inspired by TS Eliot's poem of the same name—combined the delicate and gauzy with the dense and enduring. Setting literary notion against artistic concept, TS Eliot's poem was reproduced in the promotional material and graphics used to introduce the collection to the press and buyers:

And all shall be well and
All manner of things shall be well
When the Tongues of flame are infolded
Into the crowned knot of fire
And the fire and the rose are One.

This use of poetry is typical of Georgina von Etzdorf's invitations and graphic design work, which have become as idiosyncratic and unexpected as the print designs. Poetic explanations or cards have at various times taken the shape of a bulrush, a billowing flag, a record, and a cloud. Collected and framed by some devotees, they are also in the collection of New York's Cooper Hewitt Museum, where they are cataloged under "E" for Ephemera.

Most Georgina von Etzdorf prints also play with opposites. In Blizzard, part of the winter

"DRAGONFLIES DRAW FLAME"
Invitation to view the spring/summer 1993 collection

Each invitation is conceived to convey a mood and identity. For "Dragonflies Draw Flame" the invitation was pleated to resemble bulrushes.

"SPELLBOUND"
Invitation to view the fall/winter 1994 collection

Five star shapes were riveted together to produce an irresistible invitation that could swivel to create different forms.

For "Stormy Weather" a dark,
blustery storm cloud depicted
umbrellas being blown around.

"RHYTHM & BLUES"
Invitation to view the
fall/winter 1989
collection

A musical theme was used for
the very first tailor-made
invitation. The "Rhythm &
Blues" collection inspired an
invitation cut into the shape of
a record and based on a Tamla
Motown label.

37

1995 collection, sharp, jutting peaks are combined with clouds of snowy dots; when printed in devoré, contrasts of rich pile are played off against the fine underlay. Geometric forms blend with spherical ones, smooth surfaces are juxtaposed with textured. In Horizon, from the winter 1997 collection, flickering sound waves seem to dart across the surface of the fabric. Sharp lines radiate in varying lengths and depths to give the impression of hovering lightly above the fabric. "The aim is to provide interest and contrast in combining fabrics: mat with glossy, textured with smooth, print with plain."

One collection stood apart from the "contrasts and diversity" principle. This was the "concept collection" of spring 1991, called "Blue Heaven." Here, a singular mood of the "light, airy, spider-spun, and windblown" gave an ethereal feel to all the prints. They were exhibited at selling shows on invisible wire and, Etzdorf says, "appeared to have been caught in midflight." Scarves were extended to create more languid proportions; the extra fabric immediately pushed prices up by 25 percent. "The sales in summer seasons were traditionally not so high as winter, but 'Blue Heaven' bombed," recalls Simcock. This collection taught the partners that contrasts do not only have creative and aesthetic value, bringing strength and dynamism to a collection; they also present a commercial advantage. From a retailer's point of view, lack of contrast means lack of choice.

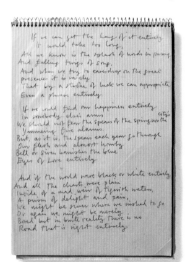

FIDDLEHEAD
Original sketch and silk stole

From poetry to poetic prints: two examples of Georgina von Etzdorf's unique handwriting, one literary, one artistic. A poem by Louis MacNeice fills an entire page of a sketchbook while, *right*, an original sketch has an almost calligraphic quality. The resulting design, based on the wispy forms of fiddlehead ferns, is shown here on a silk satin organza stole.

Sense and sensuality

PEOPLE FIND THEMSELVES drawn to the work of Georgina von Etzdorf; they become hypnotized by the colors and seduced by the textures. These are pieces that somehow work on an emotional level to exhilarate and transport the viewer. The collections both take their inspiration from an artistic dialogue with the senses and, in turn, stimulate the senses. Besides being visual feasts and tactile swathes, the prints are imbued with a musical dimension—you can almost hear the patterns.

Primal, sensory experiences, certain times of the day or year, particular qualities of light, and even smells can open up artistic channels with Etzdorf, who can be inspired to create collections purely from experiencing a mood or emotion. She vividly recalls her childhood years in Lima, Peru, with its extraordinary qualities of light and color. "I remember scorching hot sand, Lukuma ice cream, the wild Andean light, and lots of mad colors: browns and grays with wild turquoise and pinks." There were also two green parrots, called Pedro and Orlando, who would sleep on her pillow and dance to music, "and a snake in the shower who was captured and put in a bottle on the mantelpiece."

"The senses have always been my form of expression; colours speak to me, form has a rhythm," says Etzdorf. "I am totally intuitive. It's how I function—almost entirely. And intuition is fed by the senses." With lyrical, atmospheric names like "Many Moons," "Spellbound" and "Dragonflies Draw Flame," these themes and titles are the key to the way Etzdorf conveys concepts to the design team. "Whether the ideas come from moonlight shimmering on a wet road or the sound of crunching feet in the snow, a theme will travel throughout a collection and tell its own story," says Etzdorf. 'We tend to go with mood or sensory things, rather than thinking of marketplaces or customers."

COLOR GROUPS
Range of color stories for fall/winter 1997

Color is a primary tool at Georgina von Etzdorf and each collection is based on strong, defined color groups. These cards are a way of communicating color stories to designers, retailers, and merchandisers.

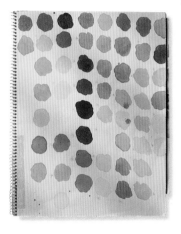

SKETCHBOOK
Color experiments, 1986

Georgina von Etzdorf's sketchbook shows an informal, instinctive approach to color which relies on gut reaction and aesthetic judgment rather than color theories or established rules.

COLOR STORIES
Spring/summer 1998

After experimentation the colors are sifted into groups, with main colors and accents or highlights.

Words are used to conjure up images and generate ideas in a suggestive, almost subconscious way, as a form of both inspiration and communication. An example is the summer 1998 collection, "A Child Went Forth," inspired by the Walt Whitman poem, *Leaves of Grass*, and based entirely on a child's perception of the world. It draws on children's experience of the earth, air, and water. The "mood board," which is used to communicate ideas to the design team, to retailers, and to clients, evokes colors, textures, and hazy memories:

Sky: Sweet pea and rose streak the sky at dusk against a backdrop of primrose, sea green, and duck egg; ethereal colors that hint at Utopia and a land of dreams. Descend to Terra Firma, sticks and stones. Sand limestone, dusty black, saffron, and lavender that break between earth and pale sky. Finally immerse yourself in the secret pool: inky blue, pale violet suggest a world sealed beneath the ice of a frozen sea … watery green, diluted aqua and turquoise peak of a heat-drenched silent lagoon.

In this collection, not only are colors used to trigger memories, but the scale of the designs is also informed by the child's viewpoint. "Children are both fascinated by detail and awed by scale," says Etzdorf, and the collection incorporates both close-ups—"as though seeing objects under a microscope"—and wide-blown spaces, represented by larger, looser prints. Fabric processes are also used to underlie the theme. Some designs are on heat-bonded, double-layered shot chiffon and printed with shimmering adhesive. This gives an extra film of color and a mysterious, glimmering underlayer of pattern, like treasures in a rock pool.

ORCHID
Design on paper,
spring/summer 1998

A fleeting impression of flowers and plants, for the collection "A Child Went Forth."

LUPIN
Cross-dyed satin devoré,
fall/winter 1997

The Lupin design on satin devoré results in shadowy graphic contrasts.

LUPIN
Printed silk chiffon,
spring/summer 1997

A design can dramatically change in character according to the colors, fabrics, and processes used. Here, Lupin is printed on silk chiffon and the mood transformed to one of dazzling light and iridescent brilliance.

LUPIN
Discharge-printed velvet,
fall/winter 1997

**When the Lupin design is
applied to a much denser
fabric it takes on a vaguely
sinister tone. Dark and
intense, the print becomes
almost specter-like, with
a haunting quality.**

43

It is usually impossible, however, to locate the inspiration for any Georgina von Etzdorf print; there is rarely any obvious link between the source and the final product. Instead, color and texture work together to bring our senses alive, transporting the pieces beyond their two-dimensional surface. "The prints have an energy and vitality that seem to refer rather than borrow. We want to create something living and vital with depth and substance."

Our world is full of color and we are constantly responding to it on a conscious or subconscious level. Our moods can be defined by color: we see red, feel blue, our expressions lighten or darken. Anyone who has felt exhilarated at the sight of an unbroken bright blue sky, or the first green shoots of spring, will be familiar with the emotional power of color. Etzdorf herself is fully aware of the way that color can click these sensory buttons. It is used uncompromisingly to startle, surprise, comfort, and arouse. "Color can unleash the senses or allow a story to unravel," she says. 'The combination of colors and how we use them can trigger things in the mind or evoke responses. It can dramatically change our moods. I believe it is color that draws people to our work, not an intellectual process."

The tactile qualities of a Georgina von Etzdorf creation are an equally important feature, as anyone who has ever felt compelled to stroke their own (or someone else's) scarf will testify. Once described as "an embrace," the delicious rayon velvets, peachy cashmeres, and furry mohairs both involve and enfold the wearer. One theory as to why the Italians took Georgina von Etzdorf so fulsomely to their hearts (well before the British) is that, culturally, they are a more sensual society with a richer texture of living. "It's very un-English to touch or want to be touched," notes Simcock. "As babies we want to touch, taste, and feel everything around us—until maturity and inhibition set in. It's not just about fashion, aesthetics, or art, it's an inner need. The world yearns for beauty, warmth, and joy."

Although Georgina von Etzdorf's work can be aesthetically challenging, it is never aggressive, always voluptuous and inviting. Like color, texture can be comforting, reassuring, and familiar, with the power to stimulate the memory and senses. "On a conscious level, every fabric carries its own history and connotations. Silk velvet has a romantic, mysterious feel that people lock into," believes Docherty. Warm, worn wools are treated so they become like cashmere; to Etzdorf they feel "like something that's belonged to me forever, since I was a baby. Some textures are so elemental they seem to come from the natural world, like sticks, stones, or petrified wood. Somehow, they are part of the landscape and become part of you." This relationship with the senses is one that links designer to wearer, and lifts the collections out of the realm of surface and image into the sphere of feeling, emotion, and experience. It is the senses, after all, that make us come alive and feel part of life.

WHILE MOST textile designers creating a collection are likely to choose a theme, visit the odd exhibition, and raid the library, Etzdorf's methods are less conventional. "One of my favorite things is driving through the countryside on a bright moonlit road with the lights off. It feels as if you are sneaking around in a strange world outside of electric light. The landscape changes into colors you can't describe, and the road becomes a ribbon of mercury." It is often these fleeting moments, which tap into a reverie of emotion and sensuality, that Etzdorf then tries to recreate in the collections. She revels in the challenge of making precious, transient moments into something enduring; of catching the elusive and trapping its essence forever. Etzdorf can linger forever watching a sunset recede or a cigar cloud develop. "An idea can start from something as simple as seeing how color fades from an ice lolly as you suck out the juice."

With such a receptive imagination there is no need to pillage books on seventeenth-century clocks or nineteenth-century architecture for images to fuel print designs. Inspiration is all around, everywhere, and is more than anything to do with seeing the world in a certain way. The sensory, domestic, but ultimately universal—common experiences that everyone can relate to—wins over the intellectual, exotic, or far-flung. The constantly changing world of nature, its seasons, and the elements are regular sources of inspiration. Water and nighttime are enduring sources of mystery for Etzdorf: "They are other worlds that are elemental and function entirely independently."

Since she was a child, Etzdorf has always been prone to casting herself adrift in flights of fancy. This, she believes, is inherited from her mother, "a highly imaginative, literary woman with a substantial inner life." As a child, Etzdorf would read fairy stories and spend many hours

ARMADA
Original watercolor
sketch

An abstract design plucked from Etzdorf's imagination. Although not originally based on any tangible subject, the final result resembles a fleet of ships.

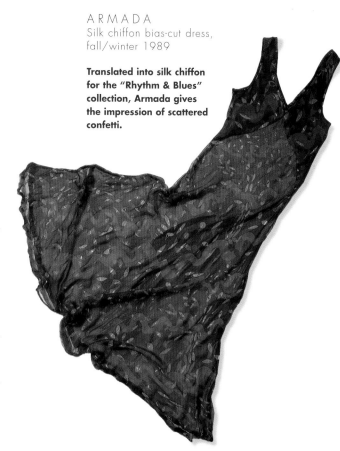

ARMADA
Silk chiffon bias-cut dress,
fall/winter 1989

Translated into silk chiffon for the "Rhythm & Blues" collection, Armada gives the impression of scattered confetti.

COMETS
Reverse-printed silk
jacquard robe,
fall/winter 1985

This frenetic design—full
of high-speed movement
and energetic brush strokes
—is reverse-printed, giving
the effect of a woven
pattern. This novel approach
came about by accident
when a pair of pajamas
were unknowingly made
up inside-out. The partners
found they rather liked
the result, and decided to
develop the theme.

gazing into the night sky. The planets, heavens, and stars have occupied many waking hours of Etzdorf's life, an interest reflected in the large number of celestial and interplanetary prints, which include Eclipse, Meteor, Comets, Star Wars, Apollo, Aurora, Jupiter, and Rockets. The partners all enjoy poetry and literature, and ideas for collections have been triggered by the poetry of Louis MacNeice, Gerard Manley Hopkins, AJ Tessimond, Victor Hugo, Alfred Tennyson, John Donne, and William Shakespeare. "At the beginning of every season," says Simcock, "I ask: 'What mood are we in?'." With its innate rhythm and ability to evoke mood or feeling, poetry is an apt springboard.

Many of the ideas behind the collections are based on common experiences and unifying images. The exhilaration you feel at the sight of a new horizon, or the giddying streak of colors you take in on a fairground ride—these are sensations and feelings that are filed away in all of us. Essentially, they are based on an openness to, and passion for, life's simple experiences. "I value the things we would instantly and naturally respond to as children," says Etzdorf. "They are spontaneous and still there, part of life when we grow up." The "Stormy Weather" collection of winter 1990, for example, was based on weather patterns and conditions, times of day and night. Prints included Nimbus, Cirrus, Tempest, and Parapluie. The "Making Tracks" collection from winter 1995 was based entirely on fading impressions: Sky Dive was

ROCKETS
Silk jacquard wool-backed shawl, fall/winter 1988

Planets and the night sky have always fascinated and inspired Georgina von Etzdorf, although references are never obvious.

STAR WARS
Silk crêpe de Chine tie, 1982

The interplanetary strand dates back to some of the earliest pieces.

48

AURORA
Herringbone linen throw,
spring/summer 1997

A development of the
Spellbound design, this
graduated degradé print
was incorporated into
the home collection.
The impression is one
of swirling mists or
the Milky Way.

APOLLO
Silk twill ties,
fall/winter 1986

A humorous print
featuring a chicken.
The name is a pun
on the Spanish for
chicken, *pollo.*

inspired by a vapor trail, Slalom by marks in the snow. Other designs took their inspiration from wolverine prints and glistening snail trails.

These rich images of everyday life are usually interpreted in a textural, sensual, and rhythmic way rather than literally or figuratively. Ideas can be triggered off by the recollection of a smell, a touch, or a certain quality of light. A typical brief that Etzdorf might give to the design team will require the powers of visual and sensual memory, imagination and creativity. "Think of how trees look when they're emerging from a mist. Think of a steamed mirror that you drag your finger across; everything's veiled behind. Think of how strange everything looks in twilight…" Ultimately, the creative process emanates from the individual and their own perception of the world. Color stories will be organized not according to trends or fashion, but in relation to the prevailing themes and moods. "I will ask the design team to recall the bizarre light just before a storm when everything is inky gray and the horizon, soon to be taken over, is a pulse of livid yellow. Or to picture balls of ice cream gradually merging in a glass bowl."

Travel is seen as a way of topping up the senses with new experiences and feelings. "I love going away because the senses come alive all over again," says Etzdorf. "It keeps your curiosity intent and your reflexes awake and alert. It's important to take the blinkers off and allow things to flow in. And it could be anywhere."

WURLITZER
Design on paper, 1984

Color and pattern can evoke mood and memories. This multidirectional repeat design recalls the dizzying excitement of a fairground ride.

PARAPLUIE
Design on paper,
fall/winter 1990

The use of dense color conjures up the menace and foreboding of storm clouds. This is peppered with the bluster and confusion of scurrying umbrellas.

PARAPLUIE
Rayon velvet scarf,
fall/winter 1990

**The depth and oil-slick luster
of rayon velvet makes it a
receptive canvas for the many
moods of Georgina von
Etzdorf designs.**

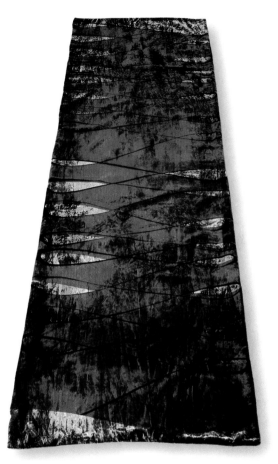

SLALOM
Rayon velvet shawl,
fall/winter 1995

**The "Making Tracks"
collection was inspired
by a variety of fading
impressions. Velvet, with
its ridging and moving pile,
was a sympathetic base
fabric for this theme.**

51

Innovation and challenge

ASIGN HUNG in the print room at the barn in Wiltshire reads: "Georgina von Etzdorf: Printed Silk Accessories." This reminder of the company's roots gives little indication of the current range of activities and developments. After 17 years of printing on a whole spectrum of fabrics, from cashmere to leather and veneered wood, and using a variety of influential techniques, this traditionally pedestrian process has been fully invigorated and energized. Many of the processes and styles initiated or developed by Georgina von Etzdorf, such as devoré, have now entered the vernacular. This has spurred the company forward, in search of new forms of expression.

Georgina von Etzdorf's move into embroidery, beading, appliqué, and "constructed" textiles is the result of an organic and natural evolution. Beading was first introduced, in a small way, with the spring 1996 "Many Moons" collection. For winter 1997's "Vive la Différence" collection, earlier print designs such as Exploding Wave and Lupin were translated into rich, glittering beads on metallic silk scarves. Using the best hand embroiderers and beaders from India, and sequin specialists in Switzerland (who produce the scintillating "schnipple" pieces using long, rectangular sequins), it is a wholly contemporary vision that propels these ancient forms of ornamentation into the millennium.

This small step from hand-printed to hand-beaded or embroidered textiles and clothing opens up a huge wealth of possibilities. The next obvious route would be to explore the vast number of traditional, largely forgotten handcrafted techniques, from faggoting to crewel work and crochet. The considered approach at Georgina von Etzdorf, however, is to take an idea, then develop it, rather than simply trot out new techniques for stylistic effect. "You can't create something by simply patching bits together; you have to nurture an idea," maintains

LINEAR SQUARE
Sequined silk georgette scarf, spring/summer 1998

One of the company's first sequin designs. The move into surface decoration represents an exciting new direction for Georgina von Etzdorf.

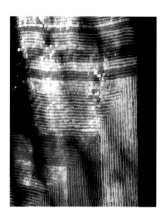

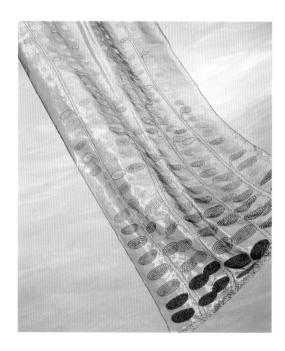

LUPIN
Silk metallic beaded shawl, fall/winter 1997

This former print design is translated into beadwork with stunning results. The subtle color graduation is a Georgina von Etzdorf hallmark.

EXPLODING WAVE
Hand-beaded metallic silk shawl, fall/winter 1997

Intricate hand-beading is combined with iridescent metallic silk to create a unique interpretation of modern luxury for the "Vive la Différence" collection.

SCHNIPPLES
Silk chiffon shawl, fall/winter 1997

Long rectangular sequins bring a new dimension not only to the fabric, but also to the senses of the wearer. With an almost animalistic life-force, the "schnipples" make the sound of rustling leaves while catching and reflecting the light.

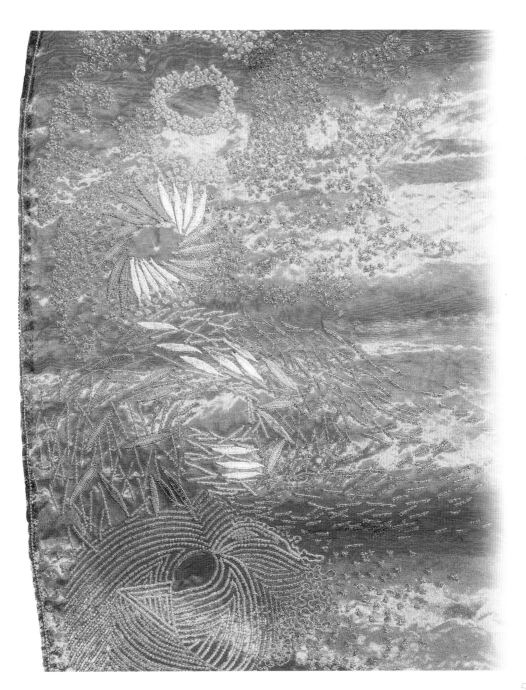

53

Simcock. The creative "bottom line" is that any technique used by Georgina von Etzdorf should serve to enhance the designs, adding depth and dimension, vitality and rhythm, color and texture. Whether recalling traditional, hand-based decorative methods or looking into the futuristic world of multi-media textiles, the Georgina von Etzdorf collections are imbued with an intuitive approach to color and instinctive feel for proportion and movement.

The realm of constructed multi-media textiles is being fully explored. Recent collections have witnessed the emergence of padded and plaited microfiber shawls, and chiffon scarves appliquéd with mohair flowers. Spring 1998 sees a buoyant range of pleated viscose scarves richly dyed and dotted with metal fishing weights. These, besides adding subtle surface and texture interest, affect the movement of the scarf, encouraging it to spring up and down and giving it a life of its own. In the same story are transfer-printed polyamide shawls with barely attached twists and swirls of polyester ribbon and dyed pheasant feathers, mounted on silk twill and stabilized with tiny weights.

Some of these ideas, including the fishing weights and the twisted ribbon designs, have emerged directly from the Research and Development department. The department was set up by Simcock in 1997 with the idea of generating new ideas outside of print design. Based somewhat incongruously in the stable block next to the Wiltshire barn, the department is a creative incubator. Working alongside textile graduates from Winchester School of Art and from Loughborough School of Art's Multi-Media course, Simcock explores unlikely materials with an open mind. "I saw Loughborough's work three years ago at Indigo, a textile design fair in Paris," recalls Simcock. "It was the most exciting collection of ideas I'd seen in years. I didn't fully understand it, but strongly believed

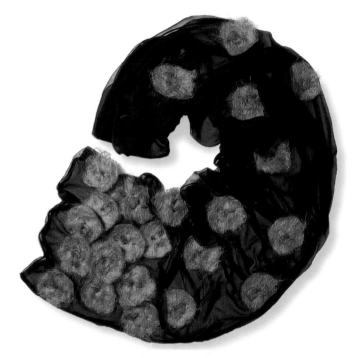

MOHAIR FLOWERS
Silk chiffon scarf with mohair embroidery, fall/winter 1997

The quest to find new ways of introducing greater dimension to designs is described by Etzdorf as "almost an obsession." Here, the application of woolly mohair to smooth silk chiffon is an unexpected combination that adds surface interest and a three-dimensional twist.

54

PLEATED VISCOSE
Scarf with fishing weights,
spring/summer 1998

**A multi-media design that
emerged from the Research
and Development department,
this light, springy creation
went on to be a great
commercial success.**

55

RUBBER AND SLATE
Multi-media design, 1995

The Research and Development department aims to nurture creativity outside a commercial framework. No idea is dismissed as too outlandish.

LATEX, STEEL WASHERS AND GLUE DOTS
Multi-media design, 1995

Latex and steel washers rank alongside silk chiffon and velvet in the R&D department.

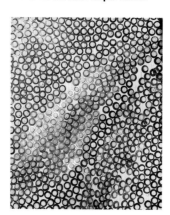

CHIFFON, SLATE AND NYLON WIRE
Multi-media design, 1996

Traditional fabrics can find unexpected companions, and produce startlingly modern results.

TWISTED RIBBON
Transfer-printed polyamide, spring/summer 1998

Twisted polyamide-and-metallic ribbon is barely attached to a base fabric of polyamide with random sequins, creating an almost airborne, fluttery effect. Another example of an innovation from the R&D department that went on to succeed commercially.

that here was the future." In this design laboratory everything is pursued, from latex studded with steel washers and pleated silk/polyester embellished with slate and nylon wire, to suede threaded with fishing tackle and chiffon looped with plastic tubing.

How marbles, plastic, or wire will work their way into the collections is anyone's guess, but the important thing is to challenge the expected and explore the possibilities. Creativity is its own reward, but can also have commercial spin-offs, introducing exciting new elements into the existing collections. And Simcock is always on the lookout for new design talent. "Someone asked me a few years ago, who is Georgina von Etzdorf's biggest competitor? I told him a second-year student somewhere in England who nobody even knows about. I want to find them and employ them... I'm constantly searching for another Georgina. I'm sure a few have already slipped through the net into obscurity."

As we approach the millennium, the challenges that face Georgina von Etzdorf, both in terms of creativity and business strategy, are numerous. The most pressing question is how does an expanding, international company maintain the purity of a craft-based aesthetic, its values and integrity? As the company has grown in size from three close friends to a tightly knit family of 50 (plus the many outworkers, contractors, agents and salespeople who form another layer of the operation), it is vital that everyone shares the same vision and is headed in the same direction. Although the company has expanded, the artistic compulsion, and thirst for the unknown, remain unchanged. "It feels a bit like we're starting again. Creatively, we are currently working on ideas that people—and even we—don't fully understand. We don't know where this journey will take us, and that's enormously exciting."

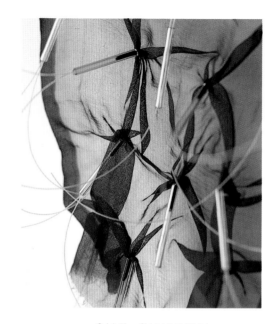

SILK CHIFFON
WITH PLASTIC
AND NYLON
Multi-media textile design, 1997

Luxurious silk chiffon is bravely melded with futuristic curlicues of plastic tubing and nylon wire.

PLASTIC,
MARBLES, WIRE
Multi-media design,
1996

Although plastic, marbles, and wire may be far removed from the sensual and embracing qualities of Georgina von Etzdorf textile designs, this may yet hold a potential idea for tomorrow's scarves.

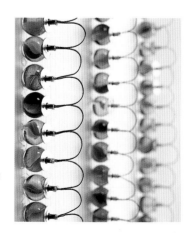

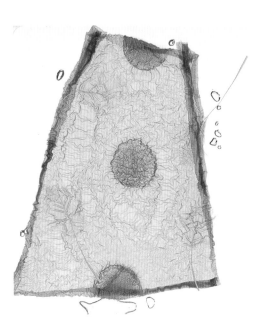

ACRYLIC BLOCK
Multi-media design, 1997

At the sharp end of creativity:
two layers of colored plastic
are fused together inside a
rectangular acrylic block.
On a lateral level, the idea of
concealment and hidden
elements could point the way
to future Georgina von Etzdorf
collections.

ECLIPSE
Printed mohair shawl,
fall/winter 1997

While the range of potential
materials to be exploited is
vast, print design remains a
focal point and an exciting
forum for experimentation.

59

Chronology

1954
Martin born 10 November, Widnes, Lancashire.

1955
Georgina born 1 January, Lima, Peru. Jonathan born 12 January, Stevenage, Hertfordshire.

1977
Georgina and Martin graduate from Camberwell School of Art, London, with honors degrees in Textiles. Jonathan graduates from Central School of Art, London with honors degree in Industrial Design.

1978
Jonathan and Martin set off on trip round the world. Martin breaks leg, returns to U.K., and builds silk-screen printing workshop at Georgina's parents' home. Georgina and Martin print first length of fabric. Martin rejoins Jonathan in India; Georgina continues printing while doing freelance design.

1981
Georgina, Martin, and Jonathan form the Georgina von Etzdorf design partnership. Sell fabric to Yuki and J.&M. Pallant. Donald Campbell uses printed wool Poppy design for dress for Princess Diana.

1983
Commit to own production. Move to converted barn near Salisbury, Wiltshire. Sell fabric to Caroline Charles, Anna Belinda.

1984
Quills, Small Dragons, Wurlitzer and Large Dragons designs. First London Designer collections.

1985
First clothing collection produced. Purgatory, Paradise, Fritillary, and Neptune designs. First cotton and rayon velvet.

1986
Retail partnership formed and Georgina von Etzdorf shop opened in Burlington Arcade, London. Metamorphosis, Comets, Solomon, and Apollo designs. Suede and leather printed for shoes, gloves, and belts. Hats produced in conjunction with Gabriella Ligenza.

1987
Cornflower, Minniver, Conversation, Jupiter and Houdini designs. First printed furniture collection.

1988
Second Georgina von Etzdorf shop opens, in Sloane Street, London. Nautilus, Zephyr, Riptide, Rockets, Bonfire, and Sparks designs.

1989
Banners, Mirrors, Scimitar designs; winter collection entitled "Rhythm & Blues." Jock Gallagher appointed chairman. Professional management drive.

1990

Designs exhibited at the Cooper Hewitt Museum's "Color into Cloth" exhibition in New York. Spring collection: "Wish You Were Here;" winter collection: "Stormy Weather." Velvet sales take off.

1991

Spring collection: "Blue Heaven;" aesthetic triumph, commercial disaster. Winter collection: "Faites vos Jeux."

1992

Spring collection: "Dancing Ledge." Winter collection: "Rhyme or Reason."

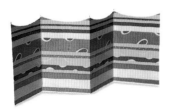

1993

Shop-within-shop opens in Barney's, New York. Spring collection: "Dragonflies Draw Flame;" first devoré design. Winter collection: "The Fire and the Rose are One."

1994

Spring collection: "Volare;" first printed satin devoré. Winter collection: "Spellbound."

1995

Sales and marketing director appointed with great plans for business expansion. Menswear discontinued. Spring collection: "Hide & Seek;" winter collection: "Making Tracks."

1996

Home furnishings collection launched. Retail partnership dissolved, Sloane Street shop closed, and Burlington Arcade shop taken over. Georgina awarded honorary Doctorate of Design by Winchester School of Art/Southampton University. Spring collection: "Many Moons;" winter collection: "Adelante."

1997

Research and Development department set up. Spring collection: "Vermilion;" winter collection: "Vive la Différence." First hand-beaded designs. Handmade "couture" section added to the scarf collection. Georgina appointed Royal Designer to Industry by the Royal Society of Arts.

1998

Spring collection: "A Child Went Forth;" includes multi-media fabrics. Winter collection: "The Prince and the Pauper." Rug collection designed for Christopher Farr. Administration move to purpose-built space with magnificent views over the Wiltshire countryside.

Index

Acknowledgments

The publishers wish to thank Georgina von Etzdorf, Martin Simcock, and Jonathan Docherty for their kind assistance with all aspects of this book.

Photographic credits
Page 9, left: Howard Sooley

All other photography by Guy Ryecart.